✔ KU-212-895

# Functional objectives

**Q1** What is a corporate objective?

**Q2** State four functions within a business.

**Q3** What is a strategy?

**Q4** Give an example of how the functions are interrelated.

# targets set by the different sections, departments or elements within a business

A1 overall target for the business as a whole

A2 marketing, operations, finance and human resource management

A3 long-term plan to achieve an objective

A4 if marketing generates higher demand, this may bring more revenue for finance; however, operations has to produce the output and HRM has to provide the staff

*examiner's* note The functional objectives are derived from the corporate objectives; once you know what the business as a whole is trying to achieve, the different functions can set targets.

( 1 ) ANSWERS

# Financial objectives

**Q1** State two possible financial objectives.

**Q2** State two possible influences on the financial objectives of a business.

**Q3** A target return on capital of 5% has been set; the investment is £200,000. What profit has to be made to hit the target?

**Q4** A target profit margin of more than 10% has been set; profits are £30,000; sales are £380,000. Has the target been met?

**ANSWERS**

# financial targets set for the business

A1 improve cash flow; improve profits; maintain low borrowing

A2 present financial position; overall strategy of the business; external conditions, e.g. competition

A3 $\dfrac{5}{100} \times £200,000 = £10,000$

A4 no; 10% of £380,000 is £38,000 so not enough profit has been made

***examiner's note*** Financial objectives may include cash flow, profits, profit margins and return on capital.

A2 **Business Studies**
Unit 3

3

# Balance sheet

**Q1** State two main categories of assets. Explain the difference.

**Q2** At the top of the balance sheet it states 'As at [the date]'. Why is this important?

**Q3** What is meant by assets employed?

**Q4** State two limitations of published accounts.

ANSWERS

# shows a firm's assets and liabilities at a particular moment in time

A1 fixed (expected to be owned for more than 1 year; also called non-current assets) and current (expected to be owned for less than 1 year)

A2 the balance sheet only shows the financial position of the business at a particular moment in time

A3 fixed (non-current) assets plus current assets minus current liabilities

A4 • out of date – refer to a specific point in time, usually in the past
• may have been window-dressed
• do not show qualitative data

***examiner's* note** The balance sheet is a financial document that all companies must produce along with an income statement. One shows all the assets of the business; the other shows the profits that the business made last year. The value of the balance sheet depends on how recent it is and the extent to which accounts are window-dressed.

# Financial accounts

**Q1** State two external groups that might want to look at a firm's accounts.

**Q2** State two internal groups that might be interested in the accounts.

**Q3** State two financial statements that all companies must produce.

**Q4** Are published accounts forward or backward looking? Explain.

ANSWERS

## statements produced by firms showing the performance of the business in monetary terms

A1 suppliers; customers; the government

A2 unions; managers; employees

A3 balance sheet; income statement

A4 backward looking; they report on what has happened, although managers will have their own projections for the future

***examiner's note*** Accounting procedures vary from country to country, which can make comparing accounts difficult. Firms will also interpret rules in different ways, so care must be taken with published accounts. The value of financial accounts depends on how relevant and up to date they are and the amount of information available on how they have been produced (i.e. which accounting policies have been used).

 **ANSWERS**

# Assets

**Q1** State two non-current assets.

**Q2** State two current assets.

**Q3** What is meant by net assets?

**Q4** What is meant by capital employed?

 ANSWERS

# items that are owned by a business

A1  machinery; computers; buildings; transport

A2  inventory (stock); debtors (receivables); cash

A3  non-current assets + current assets − all liabilities

A4  long-term liabilities + issued share capital + retained profits

***examiner's* note** The assets owned by a company have been acquired by borrowing short-term, by borrowing long-term, by money raised selling shares or by retained profits (reserves). Analysts will be interested to know what is owned and how it was bought.

(5) **ANSWERS**

# Income statement

**Q1** What is meant by 'retained profits'?

**Q2** An income statement shows a firm's assets at a point in time. True or false? Explain.

**Q3** An income statement shows the 'cash in' and 'cash out' over a period of time. True or false? Explain.

**Q4** If a firm buys £20,000 of stock (inventory) in cash, is this a cost of the business? Give a reason for your answer.

ANSWERS

## shows a firm's income and costs over a given period

A1  profits that are kept within the business rather than paid out to the owners

A2  false – this is the balance sheet; the profit-and-loss account shows the revenue and costs, usually over a year

A3  false; the cash-flow statement shows actual money flows, which may not be the same as revenue and costs

A4  no; it is a cash outflow, but it is not a cost until the stock (inventory) is used up

***examiner's* note** The income statement shows the performance of the business over the last year. This can be combined with the balance sheet to provide an overview of the firm's financial position. The value of the profit and loss depends on the extent to which the figures can be compared with previous years and with other firms.

 **ANSWERS**

# Capital expenditure

**Q1** Is capital expenditure first recorded on the balance sheet or the profit-and-loss statement? Why? Give a reason for your answer.

**Q2** When deciding whether to undertake capital expenditure, a firm might undertake an i.................................... a.......................... .

**Q3** Is spending on wages an example of capital expenditure?

**Q4** Capital expenditure may involve large sums of money. State three ways in which a company can raise long-term finance.

ANSWERS

A1 balance sheet; an asset has been purchased

A2 investment appraisal

A3 no; this is not an investment, it is revenue expenditure because the service has been 'used up'

A4 • loans
   • issued shares
   • debentures

***examiner's* note** Some firms classify research and development as a capital item and depreciate it over time. Others write it off in one go, which has a much bigger effect on profits in that particular year. Capital expenditure is important to provide firms with their key long-term assets.

# Ratio analysis

**Q1** State two shareholder ratios.

**Q2** State two profitability ratios.

**Q3** State two liquidity ratios.

**Q4** State two financial efficiency ratios.

ANSWERS ▸▸

## compares one figure with another to analyse a firm's position

A1  dividend per share; dividend yield

A2  profit margin; return on capital employed

A3  acid test ratio; current ratio

A4  stock turnover; debtor days; asset turnover

***examiner's* note** Ratio analysis focuses on quantitative data. Decisions may also take account of qualitative factors, such as the degree of risk involved in an investment, the ethics of the business and social factors. The value of ratio analysis depends on how up to date the data are and the extent to which the data have been window-dressed.

 **ANSWERS**

# Liabilities

**Q1** Distinguish between a current liability (creditor for less than 1 year) and a long-term liability.

**Q2** Long-term liabilities can be compared with capital employed using the g........................ ratio.

**Q3** State two examples of long-term liabilities.

**Q4** Which of the following is a liability: (a) stocks, (b) overdraft, (c) debtors, (d) cash, (e) premises?

ANSWERS ▶▶

# money owed by a business

A1 a current liability (creditor for less than 1 year) has to be paid within 12 months; a long-term liability does not have to be paid back within a year

A2 gearing

A3 • loan
   • mortgage

A4 (b)

***examiner's* note** A balance sheet shows all the assets and liabilities of a business at a given moment in time. The exact date is stated at the top of the balance sheet.

The amount of long-term borrowing that a firm should have depends on the cost of borrowing and how the money is used.

 **ANSWERS**

# Liquidity

**Q1** If a firm has major liquidity problems, it may be
l................................... and an a................................... or
r................................... may be appointed.

**Q2** State two current liabilities (creditors for less than 1 year).

**Q3** State two ways in which a firm can increase its cash flow.

**Q4** State two current assets.

ANSWERS

# measures a firm's ability to meet its current liabilities

A1 liquidated; administrator or receiver

A2 overdraft; creditors (payables); tax or dividends due

A3 overdraft; sell assets; chase up debtors; loan

A4 stock (inventory); debtors; cash

**examiner's note** Remember that cash flow and profit are not always the same. A firm may sell a lot of goods, but if it has not yet been paid for them, it can still have cash-flow problems. Keeping liquid is essential to the survival of the business on a day-to-day basis. In the long run, most firms want to make a profit but they have to survive in order to do this.

(10) ANSWERS

# Dividend yield

**Q1** What is the equation for dividend yield?

**Q2** If there is an increase in a firm's share price, what happens to its dividend yield? Explain.

**Q3** State two reasons why an investor might buy a share.

**Q4** State two factors that might influence the amount of dividend paid out.

**ANSWERS**

# the dividend as a return compared to the share price

A1  dividend yield (%) = $\dfrac{\text{dividend per share}}{\text{current share price}} \times 100$

A2  yield falls; the return is a smaller percentage of the price

A3  to vote and influence policy; to gain dividends; to gain from a share price increase

A4  • the overall profits      • the share price
    • shareholders' expectations      • what other firms pay out

***examiner's* note** The dividend yield can often seem quite low (e.g. 3–5%), but remember that investors also hope to gain from an increase in the share price.

The appropriate level of dividend yield depends on what other firms are paying as dividends and the possibility of changes in the share price. The yield will change regularly as the share price changes.

(11) ANSWERS

# Return on capital employed (ROCE)

**Q1** What is the equation for ROCE?

**Q2** What is the difference between the profit margin and ROCE?

**Q3** On financial grounds, would a firm prefer a higher or lower ROCE? Why?

**Q4** Why might an investor invest in a firm with a low ROCE?

**ANSWERS**

## measures the profits of the business in relation to the long-term finance invested

A1 $ROCE (\%) = \dfrac{\text{operating profit}}{\text{capital employed}} \times 100$

(where capital employed = total equity + non-current liabilities)

A2 the profit margin is the profit per sale; ROCE takes account of the total level of sales and the investment needed to generate the profits

A3 higher; this represents a higher return on investment

A4 might expect higher future returns; for non-financial reasons

***examiner's* note** ROCE is a main indicator of the success of a firm, showing its profitability. The value of ROCE as an indicator of success depends on whether profit is the objective. If firms have other objectives (e.g. social objectives), it may not be very useful.

# Profit margin

**Q1** What is the equation for the profit margin?

**Q2** The unit cost of an item is £40. The firm adds on 25% to determine the final price. What is the profit margin?

**Q3** State two factors that might determine the profit margin. Explain.

**Q4** Does a lower profit margin mean that the return on capital employed (ROCE) must fall? Explain.

**ANSWERS**

# the profit per sale (as a percentage)

A1   profit margin (%) = $\dfrac{\text{profits}}{\text{sales}} \times 100$;

     can use gross or net profit for different profit margins

A2   The firm adds on £10, so it sells at £50. Profit margin is:

     $\dfrac{10}{50} \times 100 = 20\%$

A3   the profit margin for an item is likely to be higher if it is differentiated so the firm can charge more or if unit costs fall

A4   no; if sales increase enough, ROCE may actually rise

***examiner's* note** Many candidates mistakenly think that a high profit margin automatically means high profits. Remember it is a percentage, not an amount. The impact of a higher profit margin depends on what happens to sales. If sales are maintained, profits will increase. But if the margin has been increased by reducing the quality of inputs, sales may fall and so may overall profits.

(13) **ANSWERS**

# Debtor (receivables) days

**Q1** Is the number of debtor days likely to be higher for a car dealership or a football club? Why?

**Q2** Are debtors (receivables) a fixed asset, current asset or current liability? Why?

**Q3** If the level of debtor days increases, is this likely to worsen or improve cash flow? Why?

**Q4** Why might a firm offer longer periods of credit to customers?

ANSWERS

## the amount of money owed to a firm, measured in terms of days' worth of sales

A1 a car dealership; it sells more on credit

A2 a current asset; debtors will usually pay within 12 months

A3 worsen; it suggests that customers are slower to pay

A4 to increase sales — the firm may attract more customers who can pay over a longer period

***examiner's* note** Having a high level of debtor days may be a marketing tactic, but it may cause cash-flow problems. The appropriate level of debtor days will depend on the firm's liquidity position and the type of business — furniture companies often offer long credit periods; newsagents do not.

# Acid test ratio

**Q1** The acid test is measured as a percentage. True or false? Explain.

**Q2** Is the acid test a profitability ratio? Explain.

**Q3** Stocks (inventory) £200; debtors (receivables) £300; cash £100; fixed (non-current) assets £2,000; current liabilities (creditors for less than 1 year) £500; long-term liabilities £1,000. What is the acid test ratio?

**Q4** If the acid test ratio is 0.2, what does this show?

ANSWERS

$$\frac{\text{current assets} - \text{stock (inventory)}}{\text{current liabilities}}$$

A1  false; it is measured as the number of times current assets without stocks (inventory) can cover current liabilities

A2  no; it is a measure of liquidity, not profits

A3  $\dfrac{(100 + 300)}{500} = 0.8$

A4  it suggests possible liquidity problems, as current assets without stocks (inventory) cover only 20% of current liabilities

***examiner's* note** The liquidity of a firm can also be assessed by measuring working capital, which is current assets – current liabilities.

The 'correct' size of the acid test ratio depends on the business. If the business has stocks that are likely to be easy to sell (e.g. it is a supermarket), it may survive with quite a low acid test ratio because it can always fall back on its stocks.

(**15**)  **ANSWERS**

# Asset turnover

**Q1** What is the equation for asset turnover?

**Q2** If a firm cuts price, will sales revenue increase?

**Q3** How might a firm boost sales revenue other than by introducing price changes?

**Q4** If the asset turnover increases, the return on capital employed will definitely increase. True or false? Explain.

**ANSWERS**

# the sales of a business relative to its assets

A1  asset turnover = $\dfrac{\text{sales (revenue)}}{\text{net assets}}$

A2  it depends on the price elasticity of demand — revenue will increase if demand is price-elastic

A3  increase promotion; modify the product; generate media coverage through public relations activities

A4  false; it depends on the profit margin as well

***examiner's* note** Firms will usually want to increase the revenue they generate from their assets (i.e. increase their asset turnover). The importance of increasing asset turnover may depend on the profit margin. Firms can aim either to sell more or to generate more profits from the existing sales — or do both!

# Stock (inventory) turnover

**Q1** What is the equation for stock (inventory) turnover?

**Q2** Is lean production likely to increase or decrease stock (inventory) turnover? Why?

**Q3** Why might stock (inventory) turnover decrease?

**Q4** State three problems of holding stock (inventory).

**ANSWERS**

# the number of times stock (inventory) will be used up in a year

A1 stock (inventory) turnover = $\dfrac{\text{cost of sales}}{\text{average inventories held}}$

A2 increase; less stock (inventory) is held at any moment

A3 fall in sales, e.g. the wrong items are kept in stock — people do not want them; change in policy on stock (inventory) levels, e.g. more stock (inventory) held to provide more choice

A4 may get damaged or stolen; may depreciate; involves an opportunity cost

***examiner's* note** Stock (inventory) turnover is an efficiency ratio that shows how well managers are controlling the firm. Other efficiency ratios focus on debtor days and asset turnover. Increasing stock (inventory) turnover is particularly important if a firm is pursuing a just-in-time strategy that aims for the lowest level of stocks possible.

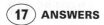 **17** **ANSWERS**

# Gearing

**Q1** What is the equation for the gearing ratio?

**Q2** Gearing 25%; long-term liabilities £200,000. What is the capital employed?

**Q3** If a firm has £2.5m of borrowing, is it highly geared? Explain.

**Q4** Why might investors be wary of a highly geared firm?

ANSWERS ▶▶

# the proportion of a firm's long-term finance that is borrowed

A1 $\text{gearing ratio} = \dfrac{\text{non-current liabilities}}{\text{capital employed}} \times 100$;

where capital employed = total equity + non-current liabilities

A2 £800,000

A3 cannot say; gearing measures the proportion of capital employed that is borrowed, not the amount of borrowing

A4 it may mean higher interest repayments, reducing profits for investors; it may mean high risk — if profits are low, this may make it difficult to make interest payments

***examiner's*** **note** Do not assume that borrowing is a bad thing. It depends on the terms of the loans and what the money is used for. The 'correct' gearing ratio depends on the circumstances (e.g. gearing is often higher when firms start up).

# Working capital
# (net current assets)

**Q1** What is the equation for working capital?

**Q2** Stocks (inventory) £100; debtors (receivables) £300; cash £200; fixed assets (non-current assets) £2,000; current liabilities (creditors of less than 1 year) £500; long-term liabilities £1,000. What is working capital?

**Q3** Calculate the current ratio using the figures in Question 2.

**Q4** Does working capital measure liquidity or profitability? State one ratio that measures liquidity apart from the current ratio.

**ANSWERS** ▶▶

# measures the day-to-day finance of the business

A1  working capital (net current assets)
$$= \text{current assets} - \text{current liabilities}$$

A2  current assets − current liabilities = (100 + 300 + 200) − 500
$$= £100$$

A3  current assets/current liabilities = $\dfrac{£600}{£500}$ = 1.2

A4  liquidity; acid test ratio

***examiner's note*** Managing working capital is important in ensuring the survival of a business. However, in the long run profitability may be more significant. The appropriate level of working capital depends on the scale of the business. A small retail outlet may hold relatively little compared to a big multinational that has much higher levels of liabilities.

**(19) ANSWERS**

# Investors

**Q1** UK investors are sometimes criticised for being short-termist. What does this mean?

**Q2** Who are auditors?

**Q3** Are investors more likely to be interested in the dividend yield or stock turnover? Why?

**Q4** Are suppliers more likely to be interested in the acid test ratio or dividend yield? Why?

ANSWERS ▶▶

# people or institutions that provide finance for a business

A1 investors demand immediate, quick returns rather than allowing managers to invest for longer-term rewards

A2 accountants who independently check a firm's accounts

A3 dividend yield; it shows the dividend relative to the share price

A4 acid test ratio; it shows the firm's liquidity and so may influence the firm's ability to pay suppliers

***examiner's note*** Most investors in the UK are institutions — such as pension funds — rather than individuals.

When firms become public limited companies, keeping investors informed and satisfied becomes especially important. Otherwise they are likely to sell their shares, which can lower the share price and make a takeover more likely.

# Investment appraisal techniques

**Q1** State two methods of investment appraisal.

**Q2** On financial grounds, is a lower or higher average rate of return more desirable? Why?

**Q3** State two qualitative factors that may influence an investment decision.

**Q4** How might the expected profits in investment appraisal be estimated?

ANSWERS

# quantitative financial methods of assessing whether or not to go ahead with a project

A1 payback; average rate of return; net present value

A2 higher; the average profits per year are a higher proportion of the investment

A3 employee morale; corporate objectives; ethics; impact on corporate or brand image

A4 based on previous experience, expert opinion or market research; relies on forecasting

***examiner's* note** Investment appraisal measures quantitative factors; the final decision will involve qualitative factors as well.

The value of investment appraisal depends on how accurate the estimates of future profits are and the extent to which conditions change in the future.

# Average rate of return (ARR)

**Q1** Total expected profit is £200,000 over 5 years; initial investment is £120,000. What is the average rate of return?

**Q2** ARR 20%; initial investment £50,000. What is the average expected annual profit?

**Q3** Why might a firm not choose the highest ARR?

**Q4** Initial costs: £120,000; expected net inflows, year 1: £40,000; year 2: £60,000; year 3: £80,000. What is the ARR?

ANSWERS

# the average profit per year compared to the initial investment

A1 $\dfrac{£200,000}{5} = £40,000$ p.a.   $ARR = \dfrac{£40,000}{£120,000} \times 100 = 33.3\%$

A2 $20\% \times £50,000 = £10,000$ p.a.

A3 may have slow payback or higher risk; may cost too much initially

A4 total profit $= (£40,000 + £60,000 + £80,000) - £120,000$
$= £60,000$

average profit $= \dfrac{£60,000}{3} = £20,000$

$ARR = \dfrac{£20,000}{£120,000} \times 100 = 16.7\%$

**examiner's note** The average rate of return can be compared with other rates of return available to decide whether to go ahead with a project. The average rate of return assesses a project in terms of profits.

# Net present value

**Q1** Discount factor for year 1 is 0.91; expected net inflow £20,000. What is the present value of this inflow?

**Q2** To calculate the present value, firms use a d.......................... f..........................

**Q3** What does the present value show?

**Q4** What determines the factor by which a future expected inflow should be discounted?

**ANSWERS**

# the discounted value of expected net inflows minus the initial cost of a project

A1  0.91 × £20,000 = £18,200

A2  discount factor

A3  future expected inflows discounted to give the value today

A4  the expected rate at which money is expected to grow over time

***examiner's* note** Net present value is one of the most complicated methods of investment appraisal, but it does recognise that £1 in the future is worth less than £1 today.

The value of investment appraisal depends on the accuracy of the projections. They are only predictions and so the risk involved must be assessed.

# Profit centre

**Q1** When managers are given authority over a profit centre this is known as d............................ .

**Q2** If a revenue target of £20,000 is set, but the actual outcome is £12,000, what is the variance and is it favourable or adverse?

**Q3** State three possible benefits of creating profit centres.

**Q4** If a cost target of £2,000 is set, but the actual outcome is £5,000, what is the variance and is it favourable or adverse?

ANSWERS

A1  delegation

A2  £8,000; adverse

A3  • may motivate staff to make more profits
    • may lead to better financial planning
    • may raise awareness of costs

A4  £3,000; adverse

***examiner's* note** A manager of a profit centre may increase profits by selling more, maintaining sales levels at a higher price, or cutting costs.

Introducing profit centres is most likely to be effective if managers can see the purpose of them, if the revenues and costs are easily identifiable for each centre and if managers have the authority and ability to influence revenue and costs.

# Correlation

**Q1** Would you expect a positive or negative correlation between price and sales? Why?

**Q2** Would you expect a positive or negative correlation between income and sales? Why?

**Q3** How can an understanding of the correlation between various factors and sales help a firm?

**Q4** What does a strong positive correlation mean?

ANSWERS

# the apparent relationship between one variable and another

A1 negative; a higher price would usually lead to lower sales

A2 positive; higher incomes usually lead to more demand for products

A3 may help to predict sales; may help to focus marketing activities on the key factors that increase demand

A4 it means that when A increases, B increases as well, and that there is a predictable link between the two (e.g. every £100 spent on advertising increases sales by £300)

***examiner's* note** Correlation does not show cause and effect. An increase in advertising may have caused an increase in sales, but the increase in sales may have provided the finance for more advertising.

Correlation can be very useful to marketing planning. If firms can identify the key influences on demand, they can try and focus on these.

 **ANSWERS**

# Extrapolation

**Q1** Past information held within the firm is called
b............................................ .

**Q2** State two reasons why extrapolating sales may be inaccurate.

**Q3** To 'smooth data' and identify the underlying trend of past data,
a firm may use a m........................... a.................................... .

**Q4** If managers do not extrapolate, how else might they estimate
sales?

ANSWERS ▶▶

A1  backdata

A2  • new technology may change the nature of the market
     (e.g. entry of digital cameras into the film market)

   • competitors may change behaviour
     (e.g. price wars)

A3  moving average

A4  hunch; use experts' advice; market research/test marketing

***examiner's* note** In order to extrapolate effectively it is necessary to
identify the underlying patterns within the data (e.g. seasonal trends).
Extrapolation is most useful when future trends follow the same pattern as
past trends (i.e. there are no major changes in market factors).

# Sales forecasting

**Q1** Sales are currently £20,000 but are forecast to grow by 10% a year. What are sales expected to be in 2 years' time?

**Q2** State two ways of forecasting sales.

**Q3** State two benefits of forecasting sales.

**Q4** State two reasons why a sales forecast may be inaccurate.

**ANSWERS**

# estimating future levels of sales

A1  year 1: £20,000 + 10% = £22,000
    year 2: £22,000 + 10% = £24,200

A2  market research/test marketing; expert opinion; extrapolation

A3  to undertake financial planning; to plan production; to undertake workforce planning

A4  competitors' actions; poor market research; market changes (e.g. new technology)

***examiner's note*** Planning ahead is an important part of most business success. Forecasting enables firms to look at where the business may be in the future and to ensure it has the resources and skills to cope with this position. The value of sales forecasting depends on how accurate it is. If it is accurate, it can help the firm plan effectively in all the other functional areas.

# Marketing strategy

**Q1** Give an example of a marketing strategy.

**Q2** A strategy focusing on a small segment of the market is called a n................ strategy. State one disadvantage of this strategy.

**Q3** A strategy focusing on the main market segment is called a m................ market strategy. State one disadvantage of this strategy.

**Q4** State three factors that might determine a firm's marketing strategy.

**ANSWERS**

# a long-term plan to achieve marketing objectives

A1  low cost; differentiation; niche; mass; local; global

A2  niche; may be limited rewards

A3  mass; may involve high costs of investing in large-scale production

A4
- its strengths
- competitors' strategies
- market opportunities
- resources

***examiner's* note** The marketing strategy is a crucial element in a firm's success. If a firm is in the wrong market with the wrong strategy, it will find it difficult to be profitable.

The marketing strategy is more likely to be successful if it fits with market needs and the firm's own strengths, if it is well planned and well executed, and if it has sufficient funding.

# Ansoff Matrix

**Q1** What is meant by market penetration?

**Q2** What is meant by market development?

**Q3** What is meant by diversification?

**Q4** What is meant by new product development?

ANSWERS

# sets out the strategic options facing an organisation

**A1** firms attempt to increase the sales of existing products in their existing markets

**A2** firms attempt to increase sales by launching existing products in new markets

**A3** firms attempt to increase sales by launching new products in new markets

**A4** firms attempt to increase sales by launching new products in existing markets

***examiner's* note** The Ansoff Matrix highlights the options open to the firm. It is up to the management to choose the right strategy for the firm. The right strategy will depend on the firm's ability to cope with risk and its ability to manage in different markets.

**(29) ANSWERS**

A2 **Business Studies**
Unit 3

# Marketing objectives

**Q1** State two possible marketing objectives.

**Q2** State two possible influences on marketing objectives.

**Q3** The target market share is 25%; market sales are £600,000. What target must your sales hit?

**Q4** Market share target is 10%; the market size is £530,000; sales are £50,000. Have you met your target?

 ANSWERS

A1  increased sales; increased market share; increased brand loyalty

A2  present marketing position; external environment; financial
resources; overall corporate strategy

A3  $\dfrac{25}{100} \times £600,000 = £150,000$

A4  no; 10% of £530,000 is £53,000 so your sales are not high
enough

***examiner's* note** Typical marketing objectives refer to sales, market share or
brand loyalty. Managers must develop the strategy and tactics to achieve these
objectives.

# Marketing plan

**Q1** How might a marketing plan affect the finances of a firm?

**Q2** How might a marketing plan affect the HRM function?

**Q3** How might a marketing plan affect the operations strategy?

**Q4** State two constraints on a marketing plan.

ANSWERS

# a detailed statement of a firm's marketing objectives, strategy and tactics

A1 may require expenditure (e.g. to launch a product); will also affect income through sales

A2 may affect the number of staff needed and the skills they need

A3 may determine what is made, when the items need to be ready and the range of products on offer

A4 money; time; skills; competitor actions

***examiner's* note** The marketing plan provides the detail of the marketing activities necessary to implement the strategy. The effectiveness of the marketing plan depends on how well it is implemented, how competitors react and the resources devoted to it.

# Marketing budget

**Q1** State three ways in which a firm might set its marketing budget.

**Q2** If the marketing expenditure budget was £10,000 and in fact the firm spends £12,000, what is the variance?

**Q3** State two reasons why a firm might end up spending more than its marketing expenditure budget.

**Q4** State two reasons for setting a marketing budget.

ANSWERS

# a quantifiable financial target for the marketing function (e.g. advertising expenditure)

A1  past levels; competitor levels; in relation to its marketing objectives

A2  £2,000 adverse

A3  • to match competitors' actions    • a change in its targets
    • poor estimates of likely spending  • an increase in costs

A4  to coordinate activities; to motivate; to limit and monitor expenditure

***examiner's* note** The marketing budget may influence the success of a marketing plan (e.g. if no funds are available to promote a new product, this will affect its chances in the market). Simply having a bigger marketing budget does not guarantee better marketing. It depends on how the money is used.

# Market penetration

**Q1** What is a 45% market share?

**Q2** How could the volume of sales increase but the value decrease?

**Q3** Why might greater market share decrease unit costs?

**Q4** Why is diversification risky?

**ANSWERS**

# occurs when a business aims to sell more within its existing market

A1 your sales are 45% of the whole market

A2 the price is falling

A3 economies of scale

A4 you are entering a new market with new products; therefore there is a high level of uncertainty

***examiner's* note** Market penetration is one strategy from the Ansoff Matrix; the others are market development, new product development and diversification. These should be considered in terms of their risk.

# Operational objectives

**Q1** State two possible operational objectives.

**Q2** State two possible influences on the operational objectives of a business.

**Q3** The capacity utilisation target is 80%; capacity is 500 units. What level must output reach?

**Q4** The capacity utilisation target is 80%; present output is 300 units; capacity is 400 units. Has the target been hit?

ANSWERS ▶▶

A1  reduce unit costs; increase volume or capacity utilisation;
    improve quality

A2  present position; corporate strategy; budget; competitors'
    actions

A3  $\dfrac{80}{100} \times 500 = 400$ units

A4  no; $\dfrac{300}{400} \times 100 = 75\%$

***examiner's* note** Operations is the core of the business; operations provides
the actual good or service and affects the quality, unit cost and amount of good
or service that can be made available.

# Economies of scale

**Q1** State two possible consequences of economies of scale.

**Q2** At the existing output of 100 units, the unit cost of production is £5. If output doubles, the unit cost decreases by 20%. What is the new unit cost? What is the total cost?

**Q3** State two types of economy of scale.

**Q4** If unit costs increase as the scale of production increases, this is known as ............................... of ................ . State two examples.

ANSWERS ▶▶

# when the cost per unit decreases as the scale of production increases

A1 • may be able to lower prices given lower unit costs, which may stimulate sales
   • if price is kept constant, the firm will have higher profit margins

A2 new unit cost = £4; total cost = £4 × 200 = £800

A3 • purchasing economies     • financial economies
   • technical economies     • management economies

A4 diseconomies of scale; communication, coordination

***examiner's* note** Economies of scale occur when the whole scale of production increases, e.g. new factories or premises are acquired. If a firm simply produces more with its existing resources, this is increasing its capacity utilisation.

Economies of scale may be essential for success if the market is price-sensitive — with lower unit costs, a firm may lower its prices and gain sales.

# Optimal mix of resources

**Q1** What is mass production?

**Q2** What is job production?

**Q3** What is capital-intensive production?

**Q4** What is labour-intensive production?

ANSWERS ▶▶

A1 producing on a large scale; usually involves production lines

A2 one-off items are produced, e.g. tailor-made suits

A3 the production process uses large amounts of machinery, e.g. production lines

A4 the production process uses a high proportion of labour relative to other resources (equipment)

***examiner's* note** The most efficient combination of resources will depend on the type of product, how flexible production has to be, the level of technology and the cost of different resources.

# Innovation

**Q1** How can a firm protect a new invention? Explain.

**Q2** Would you expect the demand for an innovative product to be price-elastic or price-inelastic? Explain.

**Q3** State two benefits of innovating.

**Q4** State two ways in which a firm might encourage innovation.

ANSWERS

# when new product or process ideas are successfully launched in a market

A1 patent; the firm registers this and then others cannot copy the invention without its permission

A2 price-inelastic; there may not be many alternatives

A3 • may develop a unique selling point
   • may be first into a market and therefore able to charge more

A4 • provide enough funding
   • do not punish failure
   • encourage employees to come forward with ideas
   • include innovation in the firm's objectives

***examiner's* note** Innovation enables firms to stay ahead of the competition, but it can be costly and take a long time. The importance of innovation depends on how rapid the rate of change is in the industry, and on the level of competition.

 **37** ANSWERS

# Location decisions

**Q1** State two quantitative methods that a firm might use to choose a location.

**Q2** State two qualitative factors that might affect a firm's location decision.

**Q3** State three reasons why the choice of location might be important to a firm.

**Q4** State two reasons why a firm may choose to move abroad.

**ANSWERS**

A1 investment appraisal; break-even

A2 • reaction of employees • quality of life
   • image of the area • ease of access to resources

A3 may affect image (e.g. perfume companies); may affect costs; may affect likely demand (e.g. hotels)

A4 lower costs; nearer the market; foreign government incentives; spread risk by having different bases

***examiner's* note** The location decision will be influenced by a range of factors, such as costs, closeness to customers, image and infrastructure. The importance of location depends on the business. It is critical for firms such as retailers and hotels that need to attract customers to their location.

# Lean production

**Q1** Through lean production techniques the cost per unit, which had been £5, is reduced by 10%. If 4,000 units are produced per week, what is the weekly cost saving?

**Q2** Lean production does not involve which of the following: (a) JIT; (b) holding stocks just in case; (c) kaizen? Explain.

**Q3** State one advantage of adopting lean production techniques.

**Q4** State three possible problems of introducing lean production.

ANSWERS ▶▶

# when a firm attempts to reduce all forms of wastage, e.g. wastage of time, materials and effort

A1 saving per unit = £0.50
total weekly saving = £0.5 × 4,000 = £2,000

A2 (b); lean production seeks to minimise stockholding costs

A3 reduces costs, which may enable more profits to be made

A4 • investment may be required to make the technology more flexible
• it may be difficult to find reliable suppliers able to deliver 'just in time'
• it may be difficult to find a flexible workforce

***examiner's* note** Lean production is increasingly important because of greater competition. It is more important to be efficient.

The effectiveness of lean production depends on the extent to which employees participate, the extent of the cost savings, whether competitors are adopting similar techniques and the extent to which employees are willing to improve quality and prevent mistakes occurring.

# Stocks (inventory)

**Q1** Are stocks (inventory) a current or fixed (non-current) asset? Why?

**Q2** Stocks (inventory) involve an opportunity cost. Why?

**Q3** State two types of stock (inventory) that a firm might hold.

**Q4** Give two reasons why a firm might reduce its stock levels.

**ANSWERS**

# goods held by a firm for use in production or to be sold

A1 current; they are likely to be used up within the year

A2 money is tied up in stocks (inventory), which could be invested elsewhere

A3 • components
 • semi-finished goods
 • works in progress
 • finished goods

A4 lean production; lower anticipated demand; warehousing costs too high

***examiner's* note** Stock levels generally have fallen in recent years due to the adoption of lean production, which aims for zero stocks.

The level of stocks held by a firm will depend on the opportunity cost, the space available, the firm's operations strategy and the danger of stock depreciation.

(40) **ANSWERS**

# Production process

**Q1** What is kaizen?

**Q2** What is just-in-time production?

**Q3** What is benchmarking?

**Q4** State one benefit of lean production.

# the way an item is produced, e.g. mass production (large-scale) or job production (one-off)

A1  a process of continuous improvement

A2  an approach that holds no stock and produces in response to demand, not anticipation of it

A3  measuring your performance against high performers as part of a process of learning from them

A4  lower costs enabling greater competitiveness

***examiner's* note** Lean production removes unnecessary costs which should enable higher profit margins or lower prices.

## methods used to prevent time being wasted

A1 simultaneous engineering

A2 kaizen

A3 may develop brand loyalty; may be able to charge more; may recover development costs more quickly

A4 • may be difficult to estimate the duration of activities, especially if the project has not been undertaken before
   • may be difficult keeping to the estimates

***examiner's* note** Critical path analysis assumes given standards and a given level of quality. If a firm lowers its standards, it may be able to complete the project more quickly.

The importance of time-based management depends on the extent to which time is wasted, the need for fast product development and the importance of being first in the market.

# Critical path analysis (CPA)

**Q1** What is meant by total float?

**Q2** An activity has a latest finish time of day 15, an earliest start time of day 2 and a duration of 10 days. What is its float time?

**Q3** What is the total float on a critical activity? Explain.

**Q4** State two possible benefits of undertaking CPA.

A1 the amount of time an activity can overrun without delaying the project as a whole

A2 LFT – EST – duration = 15 – 2 – 10 = 3 days

A3 0; if this overruns, the project as a whole is delayed

A4 • it saves time
  • it enables faster product development
  • can estimate effects of any delays
  • can prioritise key activities

***examiner's* note** Critical path analysis is part of project management and can be used for a range of projects, such as a product launch, an advertising campaign, establishing a new factory or relocation.

The value of critical path analysis depends on how accurate the predictions are about the time that each activity will take, and on whether managers can make sure these times are kept to.

 **42 ANSWERS**

# Time-based management

**Q1** Faster product development can be helped by undertaking activities at the same time. This is s.................................................... e...................................... .

**Q2** Saving time may occur through a process of continuous improvement called k......................... .

**Q3** State two advantages of being first with a product in the market.

**Q4** State two possible problems of critical path analysis.

**ANSWERS**

# HRM

**Q1** What do the initials HRM stand for?

**Q2** State two possible benefits of effective HRM.

**Q3** Why might a firm not have an HRM department?

**Q4** State two indicators of effective HRM.

ANSWERS

# the management of people at work to help the organisation achieve its objectives

A1  human resource management

A2  • more motivated staff          • greater loyalty
    • more ideas                    • lower labour turnover

A3  does not see a need; cannot afford it

A4  • low labour turnover           • low absenteeism
    • fewer accidents               • greater productivity

***examiner's* note** Firms have increasingly paid attention to the role of people in the organisation. The ability of people to contribute to a firm's competitiveness is increasingly appreciated.

Employees are more likely to be motivated to help the firm if conditions are good, the rewards are high, the jobs are well designed and employees are involved in decision making.

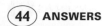

# Soft HRM

**Q1** Soft HRM is likely to be associated with d.......................... management.

**Q2** Is soft HRM likely to involve centralisation or decentralisation? Why?

**Q3** Is soft HRM likely to involve high or low levels of employee participation? Why?

**Q4** State three ways in which employees can hinder the success of a firm.

 ANSWERS

# a management approach that regards employees as an important asset of the business

A1 democratic

A2 decentralisation; managers will pass authority throughout the organisation

A3 high; to benefit from employees' ideas

A4 may make mistakes; may be slow to produce; may be rude to customers/work may be of poor quality

***examiner's* note** Employees are generally becoming more skilled and expect greater involvement in business decision making, which means they may react favourably to the soft HRM approach.

Whether managers adopt a 'soft' approach to HRM depends on the culture of the firm and managers' attitudes towards staff and their experiences of what has worked before and elsewhere.

**(45) ANSWERS**

# Human resource objective

**Q1** State two possible human resource objectives.

**Q2** What is meant by hard HRM?

**Q3** What is meant by soft HRM?

**Q4** State two possible influences on the human resource objectives of a business.

ANSWERS

# a target relating the management of people

A1 reduce labour turnover; reduce recruitment costs; improve productivity; reduce absenteeism; minimise industrial action

A2 an approach that treats employees as a resource to control

A3 an approach that treats employees as an asset to develop

A4 present performance of employees; employee expectation; finances available; culture and corporate strategy

***examiner's* note** People are an important resource but need to be managed properly; this can include fair rewards and effective training.

# Workforce planning

**Q1** State two external factors that might influence the number of employees a business wants to employ.

**Q2** Give an example of how the workforce plan is linked to the corporate strategy.

**Q3** Explain how the management of employees may be affected by the other functions.

**Q4** State two benefits of workforce planning.

**ANSWERS**

# planning human resources to ensure the right number of employees with the right skills at any moment

A1 minimum wage; employment legislation; levels of unemployment affecting wage costs; demand levels; technology

A2 a strategy of growth may require more employees; a decision to downsize may require fewer; a decision to move into new product or geographical markets may require different skills

A3 finance may determine what can be paid; marketing may determine the number of employees required; operations may determine what skills are required

A4 avoids labour shortages; ensures production can continue

***examiner's* note** Without workforce planning, managers will always react to events when they occur rather than being prepared for them. This may lead to poor and rushed decision making when it comes to staffing.

 **47** ANSWERS

# Delayering

**Q1** Delayering is often associated with which of the following: (a) rationalisation; (b) expansion; (c) correlation; (d) extrapolation? Explain.

**Q2** After delayering within a firm, is the span of control likely to be wider or narrower? Why?

**Q3** State two possible benefits to a firm of delayering.

**Q4** State two possible problems of delayering.

**ANSWERS**

# when a layer of management is removed from the hierarchy

A1 (a); involves attempts to reduce costs, e.g. removing management layers

A2 wider; each manager will supervise more people

A3 • may cut costs (e.g. fewer managers)
   • may speed up decision making by reducing the time taken for messages to go from the top to the bottom of the organisation

A4 • may be resisted by employees who fear they will lose their jobs
   • may demotivate staff due to redundancies

***examiner's* note** Delayering may meet with a lot of resistance because it involves redundancies; even those left with a job may worry whether they will keep it in future. Delayering is most likely if there is a need to reduce costs and if communication from top to bottom has been slow.

 **48** **ANSWERS**

# Employer/employee relations

**Q1** Entrusting an employee with a task is called d............................. .
State two benefits of this.

**Q2** An organisation that represents employees in the workplace is
called a t................ u................. .

**Q3** State two benefits of good employer/employee relations.

**Q4** State two reasons why employees might resist change.

**ANSWERS** ▶▶

A1 delegation
motivates subordinates; reduces overload of superiors

A2 trade union

A3 greater cooperation; easier to bring about change

A4 • fear they will not do well in the new circumstances
  • lack necessary skills
  • do not see the need or benefits

***examiner's* note** Managers have tended to pay a lot more attention to employer/employee relations in recent years, appreciating the benefits of greater employee involvement. Relations are likely to be better if employees are kept informed, treated fairly and provided with a good quality of working life.

# Trade unions

**Q1** State two factors that might determine union power.

**Q2** State four factors that might determine union membership.

**Q3** State two reasons for not joining a union.

**Q4** State two benefits that union membership might offer members.

ANSWERS

# organisations of employees formed to represent their interests

A1
- legal rights
- skill of negotiators
- number of members
- availability of labour

A2
- legal protection
- past success
- ease of organising union activities
- management attitude

A3  membership fees; may not agree with its actions

A4  bargaining power; legal advice; finance

***examiner's note*** Trade unions have decreased in influence in recent years, but with millions of members they remain a significant force in the workplace.

Managers are more likely to meet with union officials if the union has many members, the union has strong legal protection, and cooperation has proved beneficial in the past.

# Corporate objectives

**Q1** What is the link between objectives and strategy?

**Q2** State two features of a good objective.

**Q3** What is a functional objective?

**Q4** What influences the corporate objective?

**ANSWERS**

# the targets for the business as a whole

A1 the strategy is the long-term plan to achieve the objectives

A2 specific; measurable; agreed with those who have to achieve it; realistic; has a clear date by when it has to be achieved (time-specific)

A3 a target for a particular section of the business such as marketing, HR or operations

A4 present position of the business; external environment such as competitors and the economy; strengths and weaknesses of the business; aims of the owners

***examiner's* note** Setting the corporate objectives determines where the organisation as a whole is headed. These decisions should be made by the directors; the managers then have to achieve the objectives if possible.

 **(51) ANSWERS**

# Mission

**Q1** What is the difference between a strategy and an objective?

**Q2** The mission should reflect the values and attitudes of the organisation, i.e. its corporate c........................ . Why?

**Q3** State two possible benefits to an organisation of introducing a mission statement.

**Q4** What is the difference between an objective and a mission?

ANSWERS

# the overall purpose and values of the organisation

A1 the strategy is a long-term plan to implement the objective

A2 culture; otherwise it will have limited impact because employees will not believe in it

A3 • may provide employees with a sense of direction
   • may co-ordinate activities
   • may help managers to decide how to act in a certain situation

A4 an objective is quantifiable and more specific than the mission

***examiner's* note** A mission statement is useful only if it is supported by the actions of managers and the allocation of resources; otherwise it is just words. The value of a mission statement depends on whether it reflects reality (i.e. do employees believe in it?), whether it motivates and inspires, and whether it helps managers decide what to do.

# Stakeholders

**Q1** State three stakeholder groups.

**Q2** State three possible employee objectives.

**Q3** Give an example of where stakeholder objectives may conflict with each other.

**Q4** Give an example of where stakeholder objectives may coincide with each other.

ANSWERS ▶▶

# individuals or groups that affect and are affected by a firm's activities

A1
- employees
- suppliers
- shareholders
- community

A2
- job security
- career development
- fair pay and conditions
- good working conditions

A3 higher rewards for employees may reduce rewards for shareholders

A4 providing a better service for customers may mean sales and profits increase

***examiner's note*** In recent years there has been increasing pressure on firms to pay attention to their stakeholders. The extent to which a firm tries to meet the needs of a particular stakeholder group depends on the power of the group and the seriousness of any action stakeholders might take (e.g. strike or withdrawing supplies).

# Stakeholder perspectives

**Q1** All stakeholders are shareholders. True or false?

**Q2** All shareholders are stakeholders. True or false?

**Q3** State two possible objectives of investors.

**Q4** State two possible objectives of suppliers.

ANSWERS

A1 false

A2 true

A3 dividends; an increase in share price; the ability to influence the business decisions

A4 to be paid promptly; to have long-term contracts; to be kept informed

*examiner's* note The objectives of some stakeholders can overlap e.g. better treatment of staff may improve performance and profits for shareholders; objectives may clash e.g. more dividends to investors may reduce the rewards available to employees.

# Stakeholder mapping

**Q1** State two benefits of involving stakeholders in decision making.

**Q2** How might individual employees gain more stakeholder power?

**Q3** How might managers respond to a stakeholder group with little power and interest in the business?

**Q4** How might managers respond to a stakeholder group with considerable power and interest in the business?

**ANSWERS**

# a way to assess the relative power and interest of different stakeholder groups

**A1** reduces resistance; helps highlight any flaws in a plan; gains stakeholders' cooperation, which may boost the plan's success

**A2** by joining together (e.g. in a trade union)

**A3** they might ignore or pay little attention to this group

**A4** they would want to ensure this group is always informed about developments; managers may consult the group before putting a plan into practice

***examiner's* note** Not all stakeholders are equal, and not all are likely to be treated in the same way. Some stakeholders have more power than others; stakeholders may vary in how much interest they have in what a business does. Any action managers take will be influenced by the relative power and interest of each group.

 **ANSWERS**

# External environment

**Q1** What is meant by economic policy?

**Q2** State two ways in which a recession might affect a business.

**Q3** State two ways in which low interest rates might affect a business.

**Q4** State two ways in which high unemployment might affect a business.

ANSWERS ▶▶

# factors outside the control of the business (e.g. macroeconomic factors)

A1 tools used by the government to try and control the economy (e.g. fiscal and monetary policy)

A2 • may reduce demand
   • may make resources cheaper and more widely available

A3 • may decrease the cost of borrowing and increase investment
   • may increase customers' willingness to borrow and so increase demand

A4 may make it easier to recruit employees; may depress wages

*examiner's* **note** The external environment is often categorised under headings such as PEST: political, economic, social and technological factors.

The impact of external change depends on what the change is, whether the business has prepared for it, and the duration of the change.

# External change

**Q1** State two possible causes of external change.

**Q2** State two reasons why people resist change.

**Q3** State two ways of bringing about change.

**Q4** State one disadvantage of forcing people to change.

ANSWERS

# change brought about by factors outside the business

A1 changes in the law, in society, in technology and in the economy

A2 people like things the way they are; they don't see the point; they think there is a better option; they they think they will be worse off

A3 educate; coerce; lead by example; bargain; negotiate

A4 people may resent it and revert to their old ways once you stop monitoring

***examiner's* note** The right way to manage change will depend on factors such as the speed at which change is required, the risk involved, the likely resistance and the extent to which commitment is necessary.

 **ANSWERS**

# Economic policy

**Q1** State and explain two types of economic policy.

**Q2** State three government objectives.

**Q3** What is inflation measured by? State two causes of inflation.

**Q4** What is national income measured by? Define a boom.

ANSWERS ▶▶

# efforts by the government to control the economy in order to achieve its objectives

A1 • fiscal – government spending and taxation
   • monetary – interest rates and control of the money supply

A2 • high growth          • low unemployment
   • low inflation        • a favourable trade position

A3 retail price index or consumer price index; demand-pull inflation due to excess demand, cost-push inflation due to an increase in costs

A4 gross domestic product; fast growth in GDP

***examiner's* note** One problem of economic policy is timing. By the time the government has intervened and its policies have taken effect, the original problem may either have disappeared or have got a lot worse.

The most appropriate economic policy will depend on the government's objectives.

# Business or economic cycle

**Q1** State four stages of the business cycle.

**Q2** Which of the following is likely to increase national income —
lower interest rates or higher tax? Explain.

**Q3** Which of the following is likely to increase national income —
lower government spending or a weaker pound? Explain.

**Q4** What is meant by a cyclical business? Give an example.

ANSWERS

A1  boom; recession; slump; recovery

A2  lower interest rates; these encourage borrowing and spending, and discourage savings

A3  a weaker pound; this makes exports cheaper in foreign currencies, which should increase demand for UK goods and services

A4  a business where demands fluctuates with the business cycle (e.g. in the construction industry)

***examiner's* note** To try and offset the effects of the business cycle, the government may use fiscal and/or monetary policy.

Some firms are more vulnerable to changes in GDP than others (e.g. the construction industry compared to the paper industry). It depends on the income elasticity of demand for the firm's products.

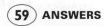

# Recession

**Q1** What is fiscal policy?

**Q2** State two possible fiscal actions aimed at boosting demand in the economy.

**Q3** What are two ways in which a business might react to a recession?

**Q4** In order to increase demand in the UK economy, would the Bank of England decrease or increase the interest rate? Explain your answer.

**ANSWERS**

a temporary depression in economic activity or prosperity (with at least two quarters in a row showing a fall in national income)

A1 a government's long-term plan for its finances, especially its spending and tax revenues

A2 increase government spending and/or cut taxation rates

A3 could cut costs; could mothball production plant(s); could look for export markets; could launch lower-priced product range

A4 it would lower the interest rate to encourage borrowing and spending

***examiner's* note** In the recession that affected the UK in 2008–09, the Bank of England cut borrowing; however, this failed to boost demand sufficiently. The bank then pumped money into the UK economy in a measure referred to as 'quantitative easing'.

# Inflation

**Q1** How is inflation generally measured?

**Q2** What is happening to prices when there is deflation?

**Q3** State two possible causes of inflation.

**Q4** State two possible effects of deflation on a business.

ANSWERS

# a sustained increase in the general price level

**A1** retail price index or consumer price index; these measure changes in the price of a basket of goods over time

**A2** there is a fall in prices or the consumer price index

**A3** • too much demand (demand pull)
  • an increase in costs (cost push)

**A4** • may lead to a fall in sales as customers delay spending in case prices fall further
  • firms may cut back on stocks in case they fall in value

***examiner's* note** To reduce demand-pull inflation the government may increase interest rates, increase taxes or decrease government spending.

The impact of inflation depends on the rate, whether or not it is expected and the cause. Demand-pull inflation is likely to mean shortages whereas cost-push inflation may lead to redundancies.

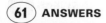 **ANSWERS**

# Globalisation

**Q1** State two reasons for selling abroad.

**Q2** State two possible problems of selling abroad.

**Q3** All countries in the European Union use the euro currency. True or false?

**Q4** State one barrier to trade.

ANSWERS

A1 access a new market; access a bigger market; domestic market is declining

A2 exchange rates; costs of entering a new market; cultural differences

A3 false; many do but not all (e.g. the UK does not)

A4 tariffs; quotas

*examiner's* **note** Some markets are more global than others — petrol may be similar all over the world whereas magazines and newspapers may have to be adapted for specific markets.

# Exchange rate

**Q1** If the value of the euro in terms of other currencies decreases, has the euro appreciated or depreciated? Explain your answer.

**Q2** Which represents the stronger value for the euro:
(a) 1 euro = $1; (b) 1 euro = $2? Why?

**Q3** How might an increase in the UK exchange rate affect a UK firm?

**Q4** How might an increase in interest rates affect the exchange rate?

ANSWERS

# measures the price of one currency in terms of another

A1 depreciated; it is worth less

A2 (b); it costs more dollars to buy 1 euro

A3 may make it more difficult to export, as UK goods become more expensive in terms of a foreign currency; makes it cheaper to import, as the UK currency buys more abroad

A4 higher interest rates tend to attract investors from abroad, leading to an increase in the exchange rate

***examiner's* note** Many firms both import materials and export goods, so exchange rates can affect them in many ways. Remember too that there are lots of different exchange rates, e.g. euro-to-dollar; euro-to-yen. The impact of a change in the exchange rate depends on whether a firm exports, imports or both and on the extent of the change.

# European Union (EU)

**Q1** All firms within the EU have to pay the same corporation taxes. True or false? Explain.

**Q2** What is a tariff? Why introduce it?

**Q3** What is a quota?

**Q4** State two benefits for British firms of the UK being a member of the EU.

ANSWERS

# a group of European countries in which there is free trade for members and a common external tariff

**A1** false; it is up to each government to decide on its taxes (except for tariffs)

**A2** a tax placed on foreign goods being imported into the country; to protect domestic firms

**A3** a limit on the number of units exported from a particular area or region that are allowed into a country

**A4** • easier to trade within the EU (no barriers)
    • access to more customers, bringing economies of scale

***examiner's* note** Many students seem to think that the UK has not joined the EU. Do not make this mistake! In fact the UK has been a member for many years.

The value of being a member of the EU depends on how much trade a firm does with member countries as compared to countries outside the EU.

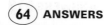

# International competitiveness

**Q1** State two influences on a firm's international competitiveness.

**Q2** Why would an exporter prefer its country's currency to be weak?

**Q3** A UK firm sells goods with a price of £200 to American customers. Calculate the change in the dollar price if the exchange rate changes from $1.6:£1 to $1.7:£1.

**Q4** How might a firm's productivity affect its international competitiveness?

ANSWERS ▶▶

# the ability of an organisation to offer better value for money than other firms competing in world markets

**A1** the exchange rate; unit costs; quality

**A2** this makes the currency cheap to buy, which means the firm's products are more price-competitive abroad

**A3** was $320, now $340, change in price $20

**A4** the higher the productivity, the lower unit costs are likely to be and therefore the lower the price at which items can be sold

***examiner's* note** International trade and the need to be internationally competitive have increased with the reduction in barriers to trade and the opening up of markets such as eastern Europe and China, which have increased competition in world markets.

The impact of a change in exchange rates on a firm's international competitiveness depends on the price elasticity of demand for its products.

 **65 ANSWERS**

# Interest rates

**Q1** A government is likely to increase interest rates in which of the following situations: (a) when demand is low; (b) when demand is high; (c) when unemployment is high? Explain.

**Q2** Interest rates in the UK are set by the M...................... P........................ C............................ . What is the goal of this organisation?

**Q3** State two ways in which high interest rates may affect businesses.

**Q4** Higher interest rates are likely to increase savings. Why?

ANSWERS

# the cost of borrowing money and the reward for saving

**A1** (b); high interest rates may reduce spending and demand-pull inflation

**A2** Monetary Policy Committee; to control inflation

**A3** • may increase the costs of repaying loans
• may reduce demand due to the higher cost of borrowing

**A4** the returns will be higher

***examiner's* note** Don't confuse interest rates and exchange rates. Interest rates are the cost of borrowing money; exchange rates are the price of one currency in terms of others. They can be related (e.g. higher UK interest rates may increase demand for the UK currency and raise the UK exchange rate), but they are different things.

The impact of an increase in interest rates on a firm depends on how much rates increase, how much the firm has borrowed and whether customers usually borrow to buy the firm's products.

# Fiscal policy

**Q1** State two types of employment law that might affect business.

**Q2** State one tax that could affect business.

**Q3** What is meant by monetary policy?

**Q4** Why does the government try to control business behaviour?

# changes in government spending and taxation rates to affect the economy

**A1** those that prevent age, race and gender discrimination; those that give employees rights concerning redundancy, dismissal, maternity and paternity and union membership

**A2** income tax affecting spending and the desire to work; VAT affecting prices

**A3** controlling interest rates and the money supply to influence spending in the economy

**A4** to prevent businesses exploiting the consumer and other businesses; to prevent the production of unsafe or undesirable products

***examiner's* note** The government helps shape the environment in which businesses operate; this can create opportunities (e.g. the government is a big buyer in some markets) and threats (e.g. new laws may limit your behaviour).

 **ANSWERS**

# Monetary policy

**Q1** If the government wants to boost demand in the economy, should it increase or decrease interest rates? Why?

**Q2** Which organisation determines the interest rate in the UK?

**Q3** State four types of borrowing that a consumer might pay interest on.

**Q4** An increase in interest rates is more likely to adversely affect a highly g..................... firm. Give the equation.

ANSWERS

A1  decrease; this will encourage borrowing because it is less expensive and discourage saving because the rewards are lower

A2  the Monetary Policy Committee — an independent body

A3  loans; mortgages; overdrafts; credit cards

A4  geared; gearing (%) $= \dfrac{\text{long-term liabilities}}{\text{capital employed}} \times 100$

***examiner's* note** In the UK, the government has given control of the interest rate to an independent body, the Monetary Policy Committee, whose present target is to keep inflation around 2%.

High interest rates are especially damaging to a firm if it has a high proportion of borrowing and/or its products are usually bought on credit or with loans.

# Supply side policies

**Q1** State two factors that influence the number of people who want to work.

**Q2** State two factors that influence the number of business start ups.

**Q3** State two factors that influence the level of investment in the economy.

**Q4** State two ways managers can increase productivity.

**ANSWERS**

# policies by the government to increase supply of goods and services in the economy

A1 the benefits paid to the unemployed; the tax rate if you are working; the wages on offer; the number of people of working age

A2 regulations on starting a business; availability of finance; levels of demand in the economy

A3 interest rates; expectations of future demand and costs

A4 increase motivation; improve training; improve equipment

***examiner's* note** Increasing supply may help the economy to grow but if the economy is in a recession, boosting demand might be the priority.

# Competition law

**Q1** Under UK competition law, monopolies are illegal. True or false? Explain your answer.

**Q2** When a group of firms collude, this is called a c...................... . How might collusion affect a consumer?

**Q3** State one possible benefit of competition law for consumers.

**Q4** State one possible benefit of competition law for UK firms.

ANSWERS

A1 false; they may be investigated, but are not automatically
assumed to be illegal

A2 cartel; may lead to higher prices and a poorer-quality service

A3 may prevent exploitation and lead to lower prices

A4 may protect some firms from predatory pricing or monopoly
power

***examiner's* note** Competition law protects both consumers and firms;
after all, firms buy goods and services from other organisations, so they are
customers too. The impact of competition law depends on the extent to which
a firm has to change its behaviour.

# Employment law

**Q1** Which of the following is unrelated to employment law: (a) the minimum wage; (b) maternity leave; (c) the retail price?

**Q2** Are the following statements true or false in the case of the UK: (a) trade unions are illegal; (b) it is illegal to make someone redundant; (c) employees cannot work over 40 hours a week?

**Q3** State two employment laws.

**Q4** How might employment laws benefit a firm?

ANSWERS

# legal obligations on firms and employees regarding employees' time at work

A1 (c)

A2 (a) false; (b) false; (c) false

A3 the Race Relations Act; the Sex Discrimination Act; the Redundancy Payments Act; the Equal Pay Act

A4 may mean a more motivated workforce, as employees feel more secure; may mean more people to choose from (e.g. if not discriminating)

***examiner's* note** UK employment laws may impose similar conditions on all firms in the UK, but there can be significant differences in the laws between countries. This can lead to differences in costs and the way in which people are treated.

The impact of an employment law depends on what the law covers and how the firm was acting previously, e.g. it may already have been paying more than the minimum wage.

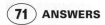

# Demographic factors

**Q1** State two factors that might affect the size of the population.

**Q2** What is the approximate size of the UK population?

**Q3** State one problem an ageing population might create for a business.

**Q4** State two reasons why the UK population is ageing.

ANSWERS

# factors related to the population such as population size and age structure

A1 birth rate; death rate; net immigration

A2 around 61 million in 2009; projected to rise to 65 million by 2018

A3 higher pension costs; may reduce demand for some products

A4 better healthcare; better diet; lower birth rate

***examiner's* note** Social factors are one element of the external environment; other elements include political, economic and technological factors and the competitive environment

# Ethics

**Q1** In order to be ethical, all firms have to do is follow the law. True or false? Explain.

**Q2** How might ethical behaviour reduce a firm's profits?

**Q3** What ethical issues could be involved in a decision to move to a cheaper production base outside the UK?

**Q4** Why might a firm behave ethically?

ANSWERS

## decisions by a business about what is right and wrong; moral principles determining behaviour

A1 false; decisions may be legal but may not be seen as ethical, e.g. you may think the firm still pays too little or it should do more for the environment

A2 the firm may decide not to trade in certain markets or produce certain products (e.g. armaments); if stakeholder groups are given better rewards, this will increase costs

A3 UK redundancies; impact on local UK community; potential exploitation of overseas labour and resources

A4 this is what it believes is right; because of stakeholder demands

***examiner's note*** Just because a firm makes profits does not mean it is ethical! Sometimes being ethical may reduce profits, e.g. if a firm refuses a particular contract. Firms are increasingly being held accountable for their actions — consumers and potential employees may take into account how the firm acts as well as what the product is like.

# Corporate social responsibility (CSR)

**Q1** What is a stakeholder?

**Q2** State two reasons why managers might act in a more socially responsible way.

**Q3** State one reason why managers may not act in a socially responsible way.

**Q4** State two benefits of behaving with more social responsibility.

**ANSWERS**

# the extent to which a business accepts obligations to stakeholders over and above its legal obligations

A1 an individual or organisation with an interest in the activities of a business

A2 more pressure from investors and society; believe it is the right thing to do; rivals are doing it

A3 costs; do not see the point or need; owners do not want this

A4 may feel better; may attract support from stakeholders

***examiner's* note** Ultimately, a business trying to be socially responsible should make decisions on the basis of what is right, not what is profitable.

# Technological change

**Q1** In what ways can technology help employees?

**Q2** How can new technology create jobs?

**Q3** Why might employees resist technological change?

**Q4** How might technological change benefit a firm?

ANSWERS

# changes in the way products are made or processes carried out

**A1** can help them communicate (e.g. e-mail), work more effectively (e.g. machinery), and make life easier (e.g. working from home)

**A2** can create new markets (e.g. DVDs) and new ways for people to buy (e.g. the internet)

**A3** may fear loss of job or status, or feel unable to use the technology

**A4** may reduce costs (more efficient) or increase demand (e.g. create a unique selling proposition)

***examiner's note*** Technology can affect all aspects of business, e.g. communication (e-mail), production (computer design), marketing (via websites), finance (spreadsheets). Technology is not just about robots!

Whether a firm benefits from technological change depends on whether it is the first to adopt new technology, the cost of introducing it and employees' reaction.

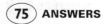 **75** ANSWERS

# Porter's five forces

**Q1** State two possible barriers to entry.

**Q2** State two factors that determine buyer power.

**Q3** State two reasons why rivalry might be high.

**Q4** State one factor that influences the substitute threat.

**ANSWERS**

# forces that determine the profitability of an industry

**A1** entry costs; economies of scale; brand loyalty; government regulations

**A2** number of buyers; size of buyer; number of suppliers

**A3** falling market; many similar-sized firms

**A4** ease of switching; how similar the benefits are

***examiner's* note** Business can take actions to try and make the five forces more favourable e.g. a takeover reduces rivalry.

# Threat

**Q1** How can a business try to anticipate threats?

**Q2** To respond quickly to change, a business might want a flexible workforce. How can this be achieved?

**Q3** To avoid being left with stock it cannot sell, a business may use JIT production. What does JIT stand for?

**Q4** To be prepared for a possible disaster, a business may have a c................ plan.

ANSWERS

# possible occurrence that could damage a business

A1 through primary and secondary market research; it is important to monitor the business environment

A2 using temporary and part-time staff; having flexi-time working; being prepared to outsource or buy in specialists when needed

A3 just in time

A4 contingency

***examiner's* note** Businesses need to anticipate threats and protect themselves against them; however, not every threat can be planned for so the business needs to consider how likely threats are and how serious they are.

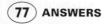

# External growth

**Q1** State one advantage of external growth over internal growth.

**Q2** What is the difference between a takeover and merger?

**Q3** Why do businesses want to grow?

**Q4** If unit costs increase with expansion, this is due to
d........................ of scale.

ANSWERS

# the expansion of a business through integrating with other businesses

A1 it is faster; may help to achieve objectives more quickly

A2 with a takeover, one business acquires the other; with a merger the businesses join together to form a new organisation with shared ownership

A3 market power; prestige; economies of scale; personal objectives

A4 diseconomies

*examiner's* note Growth is a common objective as businesses try to gain power, protect themselves from takeover and gain a sense of achievement; however, managers need to manage the speed and process of growth to prevent diseconomies of scale.

# Takeover

**Q1** What is horizontal integration? Why do it?

**Q2** What is vertical integration? Why do it?

**Q3** What is conglomerate integration? Why do it?

**Q4** Why is a public limited company more vulnerable to a takeover than a private limited company?

ANSWERS

A1 firms at the same stage of the same process joining together; to gain economies of scale

A2 firms at different stages of the same production process joining together; to gain control over supplies or distributors

A3 firms in different processes joining together; to diversify and spread risks

A4 shares are traded freely; cannot restrict who shares are sold to

***examiner's* note** A takeover enables much faster growth than organic growth, but it may be riskier. The gains from a takeover depend on which type it is (e.g. moving into a new market may spread risks whereas joining with a similar firm focuses more on the benefits of large-scale production).

# Leadership

**Q1** How might a leader be different from a manager?

**Q2** What sources of power might a leader have?

**Q3** Why might a business appoint a new leader?

**Q4** Why might people resist a new leader?

ANSWERS

# the ability to guide, control or direct others in a business

A1 a manager may focus more on what is going on now rather than in the future; a manager's job may be more about organising and controlling resources than providing a vision

A2 he/she may know more (have expert power); he/she may control resources; he/she may have charisma

A3 because the business is in trouble; because the present leader is leaving; because the business wants a new leader for a new approach

A4 they fear change; they think they will be worse off; they do not agree with the plan

***examiner's* note** A leader may be a manager and a manager may be a leader, but the two things do not always go together. A business might have a manager who does that job well but does not inspire employees or lead the business forward.

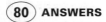 **80** ANSWERS

# Leadership style

**Q1** If employees are told what to do, this is an a................................. leadership style. State one benefit of this style.

**Q2** If managers ask employees for their views, this is a d................................. leadership style. State one benefit of this style.

**Q3** State two factors that influence the choice of leadership style.

**Q4** State two possible problems of adopting the wrong style.

**ANSWERS**

# the way in which employees are managed

A1 authoritarian; fast decision making

A2 democratic; benefit from ideas and skills of others

A3 • attitudes and skills of employees and managers
   • urgency and risk of the task

A4 • may demotivate employees
   • staff may not cooperate
   • may increase labour turnover

**examiner's** note Leaders can influence the direction of the business and motivate and inspire staff. But employees need the necessary skills and training as well.

There is no one right way of leading people. It depends on the task, the circumstances, the leader and the subordinates.

# Organisational (or corporate) culture

**Q1** State two types of organisational culture.

**Q2** State two reasons why employees may resist a change of culture.

**Q3** State two ways of bringing about a change of culture.

**Q4** What might be the consequences of a clash of cultures within an organisation?

**ANSWERS**

# the values, attitudes and beliefs of employees

A1 • innovative        • bureaucratic        • task-focused
   • people-focused     • role-focused        • risk-taking

A2 may lose status; may not understand the need for change; may disagree about the need for change

A3 educate and explain; force people to change; reward the 'right' behaviour

A4 high labour turnover, resentment, anger, poor communication

***examiner's* note** Changing culture can be a very slow process because the firm has to change attitudes that may be deeply ingrained within people.

The 'right' culture depends on the demands of the market, the priorities of customers, the nature of employees and the firm's objectives.

# Power culture

**Q1** What is a task culture?

**Q2** What is a role culture?

**Q3** Why is culture hard to change?

**Q4** Why is culture important in change?

ANSWERS

# occurs in an organisation which is very centralised

**A1** focuses on getting the job done; individuals brought in for their expertise and ability to contribute to the task

**A2** an organisation where responsibilities are clearly defined and rules and policies are common

**A3** involves changing people's attitudes, which can be difficult and slow

**A4** affects what people do and how they do it; affects willingness to change

***examiner's* note** A power culture may not be appropriate as a business grows because those at the centre cannot cope with so many decisions; they need to delegate and so a role culture may be more appropriate.

# Innovative culture

**Q1** State two influences on the culture of a business.

**Q2** Why might managers want to change culture?

**Q3** How might managers change culture?

**Q4** State two other types of culture.

## an environment in which people are encouraged to try new things

**A1** the type of business; the rate of change in the industry; the values and attitudes of the owners

**A2** to improve performance; to reduce resistance to change; to bring in new ways of doing things; because of new competition or threats

**A3** replace employees; reward those who adopt new ways; punish those who do not change; educate on the value of/need for change

**A4** team; risk taking; customer focused; bureaucratic

***examiner's* note** The culture of a business affects the way people behave, the decisions they take, the risks they take and the way they deal with others. Changing culture can be very slow and difficult because you have to change the way people think.

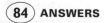

# Strategy

**Q1** The overall business strategy is called the c........................ strategy.

**Q2** A strategy is usually implemented by the use of CCTTASI. Unscramble the letters to find the word.

**Q3** State two factors that might determine a firm's strategy.

**Q4** Which of the following is not an example of a strategy: (a) diversifying into new markets; (b) cutting costs to boost profits; (c) a target of increasing profits by 30% in 3 years? Why?

**ANSWERS**

# a long-term plan to achieve a firm's objectives

A1 corporate

A2 tactics

A3 • its objectives – it needs to know what it is aiming for
   • its resources – a strategy should be built on a firm's strengths

A4 (c); it is an objective

***examiner's* note** Remember to analyse the strategy in detail. There is no point getting the marketing mix right, for example, if the marketing strategy is wrong and the market is shrinking.

The success of a strategy depends on whether it fits with a firm's resources (e.g. can the firm implement it effectively?) and how competitors react to it. The strategy will need to change over time as conditions and objectives alter.

# Differentiation

**Q1** How might a business protect a new invention?

**Q2** Is demand for a differentiated service likely to be price-elastic or price-inelastic?

**Q3** Differentiated products may have a USP. What does this abbreviation stand for?

**Q4** State two ways in which a retailer of clothes could differentiate itself.

ANSWERS

## occurs when a business aims to offer greater benefits than the competition

A1  using a patent

A2  price-inelastic

A3  unique selling proposition

A4  wide range of clothes; specialist brands; excellent customer service

*examiner's* **note** If a business aims to differentiate, it must ensure that customers will be willing to pay for the extra benefits so that the business can cover the cost of providing these benefits. Competitors may soon imitate what the business does if the differentiation proves successful.

# New-product development strategy

**Q1** State two other strategies in the Ansoff Matrix apart from new-product development.

**Q2** New-product development is an investment. What are two ways of assessing an investment financially?

**Q3** State the stages of new-product development.

**Q4** Research and development focus on understanding customer needs. True or false?

**ANSWERS**

# a long-term business plan that focuses on developing new products for existing customers

A1 market penetration; market development; diversification

A2 payback; average rate of return; net present value

A3 idea generation; screening of ideas; product development; testing; launch

A4 false; market research has such a focus

***examiner's* note** In some sectors — for example, the drug industry — new-product development can take years. However, in other sectors, such as consumer electronics, the process can be a lot faster. Product development is critical in many sectors, including the computer-game, car and film industries.

# Strategic decisions

**Q1** A firm's strategy is implemented by t...................... .

**Q2** Choosing one strategy may mean giving up another. This involves an o........................................ c................. .

**Q3** When considering a strategy, a firm may use investment appraisal techniques. State two such techniques.

**Q4** In marketing there are two main strategies: niche and mass. Explain these.

**ANSWERS**

# deciding on the long-term plan to achieve the firm's objectives

A1 tactics

A2 opportunity cost

A3 payback; average rate of return; net present value

A4 niche: focusing on a small segment of the market; mass: aiming at the majority of the market

***examiner's* note** Sometimes a firm's strategy is systematically planned and implemented. At other times, strategy emerges over time and develops gradually.

The effectiveness of a firm's strategy depends on whether it is the right strategy and whether the firm has the resources and skills to implement it effectively.

# International business

**Q1** State two reasons why a firm may start exporting.

**Q2** State two reasons why a government might welcome a foreign firm.

**Q3** State two problems of expanding abroad.

**Q4** State two ways of entering a foreign market.

ANSWERS

# a business that trades with other countries

**A1** to increase sales; domestic market saturated; new opportunities, e.g. trade agreements

**A2** it creates jobs; may lead to more tax revenue; brings skills and technology

**A3** legal differences; may not understand market; language and cultural differences

**A4**
- exporting
- using an agent
- joining with existing firm
- setting up own production facilities

***examiner's* note** Greater international trade creates new opportunities both for supplies and for export markets.

The value of international trade depends on the nature of foreign markets, the extent of overseas competition and a firm's ability to compete abroad.

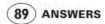

# International marketing

**Q1** What is an export?

**Q2** Why might the domestic market not be attractive?

**Q3** What is meant by a 'strong pound'?

**Q4** State two ways in which a country's government may try to prevent foreign goods from entering that country.

**ANSWERS**

# a mutually beneficial exchange process involving businesses in more than one country

A1 an export generates revenue from overseas, i.e. it is a product sold abroad

A2 too competitive; declining or slow growth; not allowed by the government to grow any more

A3 it means the pound is worth a lot in terms of foreign currency

A4 tariffs; quotas; complex administrative procedures

***examiner's note*** Overseas markets can offer new opportunities and the potential for more sales. However, international marketing does involve understanding the needs of customers abroad and developing an appropriate marketing mix; this can be more complex than operating in the domestic market.

# Protectionism

**Q1** State two examples of protectionism.

**Q2** State two reasons why a government might protect an industry.

**Q3** State two possible disadvantages of protectionism to consumers.

**Q4** State two reasons why a government might subsidise a firm to locate in its region.

**ANSWERS**

# methods of helping domestic firms compete against international businesses

A1 quotas; tariffs; regulations that make it difficult for foreign goods/services to be sold in the country

A2 • retaliation
• to prevent unemployment
• to help the industry become more competitive
• to protect the industry against unfair competition

A3 pay higher prices for goods; less choice

A4 • to encourage more firms to invest and provide jobs
• to retaliate against subsidies offered elsewhere

***examiner's* note** The world trend is towards less protectionism. The World Trade Organisation aims to remove protectionism among member countries and was joined recently by China.

The extent of government protectionism depends on the need to help certain industries, a government's attitude to intervention and the protectionism of other governments.

 **91** **ANSWERS**

# Objectives

**Q1** What is the relationship between the objective and the strategy of a firm?

**Q2** Give two ways in which setting objectives might benefit a firm.

**Q3** State two typical objectives of a business.

**Q4** What might influence a firm's objectives?

ANSWERS ▶▶

# quantifiable targets

A1 the strategy is the long-run plan to achieve the objective

A2 • may motivate
- may help to co-ordinate activities
- may help to review progress and control subordinates' behaviour

A3 • to make profits
- to increase market share
- to innovate

A4 its owners' wishes; the firm's resources and stage of development; external environment; competitors' actions

*examiner's* **note** Objectives may be forced on subordinates (which is demotivating); alternatively, superiors may discuss and agree objectives with their subordinates (which is motivating). The value of setting objectives depends on how they are set and how realistic they are.

# Corporate plan

**Q1** State two advantages of having a corporate plan.

**Q2** What is a functional objective?

**Q3** State two common business objectives.

**Q4** Why might a corporate plan fail?

ANSWERS

# a detailed statement of the overall objectives and strategy of a business

A1 • coordinates activities
• may clarify the role of each department
• may be easier to raise finance by showing the plan to investors
• helps to identify the resources required

A2 it sets out the targets for the different functions (e.g. marketing, production and HRM); these are derived from the corporate objective

A3 growth; boost profits; boost market share; survival

A4 insufficient resources, competitors' actions, changes in the external environment

*examiner's* note Planning ahead is an essential part of management. The value of a corporate plan depends on whether it is the right plan, whether the firm has the resources to implement it and whether external factors are as expected.

 **ANSWERS**

# Contingency plan

**Q1** State two advantages of having a contingency plan.

**Q2** How does a firm decide what contingencies to plan for?

**Q3** State one disadvantage of having a contingency plan.

**Q4** Give two contingencies that a firm may plan for.

**ANSWERS**

A1 • can react quickly if a problem occurs
   • reduces the danger of panic

A2 may consider the risk of an event actually happening and the extent of the problem if it does

A3 may waste resources and never be used

A4 • problems with suppliers       • a strike at the workplace
   • illness of a senior executive  • loss of major customer

***examiner's* note** The type of contingency planned for will vary from one organisation to another. A local council may plan for floods; an airline may plan for a problem with aircraft engines.

The value of contingency planning depends on how good the plan is, whether the right events have been planned for and whether enough resources have been devoted to the plan.

# SWOT analysis

**Q1** Is a high return on capital employed a strength, weakness, opportunity or threat?

**Q2** Which is a threat for a firm: (a) new competitors entering the market; (b) high profit margins; (c) lower borrowing?

**Q3** Which is most likely to be a strength for a firm: (a) low liquidity; (b) many 'dog' products; (c) positive cash flow? Explain.

**Q4** Which is most likely to be a weakness for a firm: (a) high borrowing; (b) high capacity utilisation? Why?

**ANSWERS ))**

**A1** strength

**A2** (a)

**A3** (c); positive cash flow occurs when the inflows exceed the outflows; this means the business is liquid and can pay its bills

**A4** (a); it will have to pay interest on its borrowing, which may be difficult if profits are low

***examiner's*** **note** S and W usually relate to existing internal strengths and weaknesses; O and T refer to future external opportunities and threats. SWOT analysis examines the situation but managers must decide for themselves what to do next. The usefulness of SWOT analysis depends on how effective the strategy is that follows from it.

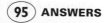

# Pressure groups

**Q1** For a firm, a trade union is an example of an internal pressure group. What might a trade union's aims be?

**Q2** State two ways in which a pressure group can influence a firm's activities.

**Q3** State two business issues that often attract the interest of environmental pressure groups.

**Q4** State two factors that may determine pressure group strength.

ANSWERS ▶▶

A1 job security, better terms and conditions, career development

A2 lobbying; direct action; boycotting

A3 • pollution emissions    • use of renewable resources
   • energy conservation    • recycling

A4 • number of members    • negotiating skills of representatives
   • financial resources    • access to the media

***examiner's* note** Some firms have invited pressure groups in to hear their views. In this way they can avoid problems later on. The way a firm reacts to a pressure group may depend on the power of the group, the views of the firm's managers and owners, and the likely seriousness of pressure group action.

# Information management

**Q1** State two features of good information.

**Q2** How does good information help competitiveness?

**Q3** What do managers do?

**Q4** Why is communication important in a business?

**ANSWERS**

# the process of gathering, processing and distributing information within a business

**A1** relevant; provided in cost-effective way; provided to the right person when it is needed in an accessible form

**A2** it helps you to understand the environment better; it helps you to understand your own strengths and weaknesses better; it can help make better decisions

**A3** plan, organise resources, coordinate, control and communicate

**A4** ensures stakeholders know what is happening and you know what they think; helps provide direction and motivation

***examiner's note*** Managing information is an important part of business these days and is particularly important as markets are changing so fast; better information on customers, rivals and the business environment can enable you to make better decisions.

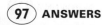 **ANSWERS**

# Decision-making model

**Q1** Outline the stages of the decision-making model.

**Q2** What are secondary data?

**Q3** State two methods of gathering primary data.

**Q4** State two quantitative decision-making tools.

ANSWERS

# a systematic method of choosing a particular course of action

**A1** a firm sets objectives, gathers data, analyses data, selects a strategy, implements and reviews

**A2** information that already exists (e.g. backdata).

**A3** observation; survey; experimentation

**A4**
- critical path analysis
- ratio analysis
- investment appraisal
- price elasticity of demand

***examiner's* note** To estimate the probability of different outcomes, a firm may look at past data, use market research or ask experts. The style of decision making may vary according to the situation. Asked to bet £1 on a horse, you may simply guess. When buying a house for thousands of pounds, you may be more systematic in your approach.

# Scientific decision making

**Q1** State two advantages of scientific decision making.

**Q2** State two disadvantages of scientific decision making.

**Q3** Some decision makers use hunch. Why?

**Q4** Ratio analysis can be used in decision making. State two types of ratio and give an example of each.

ANSWERS

# a systematic quantitative approach to choosing between alternatives

A1 • may reduce risk by allowing decisions based on data
   • can review actions and decide on the most effective course of action

A2 • may be slow
   • may lack creativity/fail to lead to innovative and different approaches

A3 data are not available, hunch enables a quick decision

A4 • liquidity (e.g. acid test)
   • efficiency (e.g. stock or inventory turnover)
   • profitability (e.g. return on capital employed)
   • shareholder ratios (e.g. dividend yield)

***examiner's* note** The data for scientific decision making can be gathered using primary or secondary research. Scientific decision making is most likely to be useful if the data are up to date and relevant, and if they are analysed effectively.

# Decisions

**Q1** What is a strategic decision?

**Q2** What is a tactical decision?

**Q3** Why do decisions involve an opportunity cost?

**Q4** What is scientific decision making?

ANSWERS

# choosing between alternatives

A1 this is long term, involving a large commitment of resources; involves high risk and is difficult to reverse; likely to be made at a senior level

A2 this is short term; often a decision that has been made before; usually made at a low level; relatively easy to reverse

A3 if you choose one course of action, you are sacrificing the alternative

A4 logical, rational decision making based on data (as opposed to gut feeling)

*examiner's* note Making decisions lies at the heart of management. Managers are continually deciding what to do and the best way of doing it. They must set objectives and decide on the best way to achieve these given the constraints and alternatives involved.